To Dexter,

Embrace your inner giraffe!

Your friend,
Chris Peters

A New Home for LoLo

MOVING INTO THE OMAHA ZOO'S AFRICAN GRASSLANDS

BY CHRIS PETERS • PHOTOS BY MEGAN FARMER, BRENDAN SULLIVAN AND KENT SIEVERS
OF THE OMAHA WORLD-HERALD

Today is moving day at the zoo.

Cheetahs, elephants, zebras and more.
They're all settled into their homes in the new grasslands exhibit.

All of the animals have come outside
to meet their new neighbors for the first time.
But LoLo, the zoo's littlest giraffe, has dug her feet in the ground.
She wasn't going to budge.

LoLo watched her giraffe family walk out of their barn one by one.
They each started across the sidewalk toward a big, green yard with trees.

LoLo's mother nudged her. It was her turn.
She raised her eyebrows, and her knees wobbled.
She stumbled backward and stomped around nervously, as giraffes do.

She didn't want to meet her new neighbors. They sounded scary.

"LoLo," her mother said. "I know it might sound frightening, but it'll be fun.
Remember your old yard?"

LoLo did remember her old yard.
She missed her old friends, the ostriches and spur-winged geese.

So she moved her hooves forward and stepped outside.

She saw rock formations, a watering hole and a straw-covered African lodge.
Everything had changed. It was all new. And that was scary.

She turned her long, spotted neck and looked around.
Down the hill was the biggest animal she had ever seen.
It was an African elephant with floppy ears,
a droopy trunk and thick, white tusks.

LoLo shuffled her hooves and stepped back inside the building.

A trumpeting sound shook inside LoLo's ears.
"Hey, LoLo!" she heard echoing from down the hill. "Lo-o-o-o-oLo?"

She peeked her furry face back out the door.

"It's going to be OK," the elephant shouted.
"I had to move too, all the way from Africa."

LoLo took a step forward to listen.

The elephant told LoLo how her family got to the zoo. She said their land was drying up. The zoo's veterinarians brought them food and took care of them.

One day, the elephants boarded a plane for America. It was a long flight, almost halfway around the world, but when they finally got to the zoo, the elephants had a brand new building and a yard just like LoLo's.

"You can do it, LoLo!" the elephant shouted.

LoLo took a couple more steps forward.

Even farther in the distance, she saw the elephants' new neighbors.
There were white-and-black striped zebras and an animal
that looked like a deer, only with long, twisting black horns.

"What's that?" LoLo asked her mother.

"That's an impala," her mother said.
"You get to play with impalas in your yard, too."

LoLo stepped back.

LoLo felt two fuzzy little giraffe horns — called ossicones —
nudge her in the back. It was her big sister Bailey.

Bailey pointed her neck toward the group of cute little
deer-like animals in her own yard. They didn't have any horns.

"Those are our new friends, the impalas" Bailey said.
"They're all girls, and they don't have horns."

Maybe it would be OK after all, LoLo thought.

The two sisters joined the parade of giraffes walking down the path.
But then, just as LoLo reached the end of the walkway,
she saw a rhino in the distance.

It was huge. It had scratchy gray skin and two sharp horns.
LoLo saw one of the little impalas prancing around near the giant rhino
and its family. The rhino looked at the impala and charged forward.
The impala ran away. LoLo took a step back.

LoLo peeked through the branches
and saw the impalas bouncing toward her.
They jumped high and moved across the grass like ballerinas.

"Why did the rhino do that?" LoLo asked the impala family.

The impalas crowded together near the end of the yard,
staring straight at LoLo.

"Marina the rhino likes to charge," one of the impalas said.
"It can be scary, but that's OK. It happens all the time."

"Why do you keep going over there?" LoLo asked.

"Because," the little impala said. "It's fun to play around.
She doesn't mean harm. It's just what rhinos do."

LoLo took two steps forward.

LoLo was almost there.
All of the other animals came forward to greet her and her giraffe family.

There were white storks, who like to eat fish with their long, orange beaks.
And, of course, the loud, honking spur-winged geese, LoLo's old friends.

LoLo's legs kept moving forward.

Before she knew it, her hooves touched grass.
She had made it.

LoLo had met all of her new neighbors, except one.
Big, flapping ostriches were the last animals to move
into their new home at the zoo. LoLo could see that the huge,
long-necked birds were unsure about the move.

LoLo thought about her day, and she thought about the new friends
she had made along the way. She remembered how nice all of them were
and how they had helped her when she was most afraid.

So LoLo walked up to the ostriches with a smile on her face.
"Here," she said. "I'll show you the way."

Omaha's Henry Doorly Zoo & Aquarium
African Grasslands Exhibit

The 28-acre Suzanne & Walter Scott African Grasslands was completed in spring 2016 after two years of construction. The savanna exhibit stretches across the entire south end of the Henry Doorly Zoo & Aquarium, reaching to the zoo's easternmost point. It's a $73 million project with exhibits designed to imitate natural African habitats. Instead of living only with their own species, many animals share the same yard, just as they do in the wild. The project saw the reintroduction of African elephants and plains zebras to the zoo.

Dennis Pate
Zoo Director and CEO

The African Grasslands is the first big step in a total redesign of the zoo. The zoo's CEO and executive director, Dennis Pate, has envisioned a master plan that calls for replacing some exhibits — those grouped by the type of animal — with exhibits that mix animals based on their native region in the world. Future plans call for areas named Asian Highlands, Coastal Shores, Equatorial Africa and more.

In 2014, travel website TripAdvisor named Omaha's zoo the world's best zoo in its Travelers' Choice awards. The attraction began as Riverside Park, a city park founded in 1894. The Omaha Zoological Society was organized in 1952 to help improve conditions for the animals, and in 1963, Margaret Hitchcock Doorly donated $750,000 to the zoo with the stipulation that the zoo be named for her late husband, Henry Doorly, publisher of The World-Herald. The zoological society was reorganized in 1965 to run the zoo as a nonprofit organization.

Improvements and growth continued over the years, as the zoo added the Cat Complex, Mutual of Omaha's Wild Kingdom Pavilion, Lied Jungle, Scott Aquarium and the Lozier IMAX Theater. Most of that growth was overseen by Dr. Lee "Doc" Simmons, the zoo's widely respected director from 1970 to 2009. Other exhibits have followed, including the Desert Dome, Kingdoms of the Night and Expedition Madagascar. Growth and development will continue into the future.

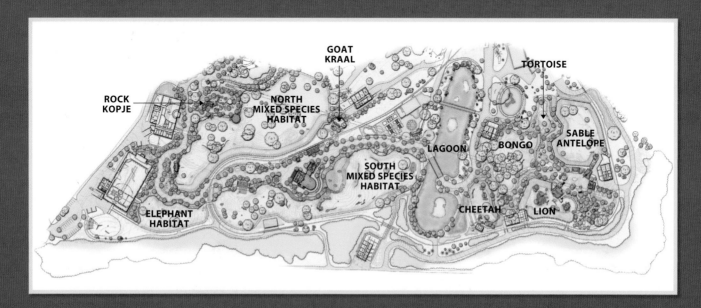

Elephants came a long way to Omaha

The zoo's six new African elephants had quite a journey to Omaha. The elephants were forced to leave their home in two wildlife parks in the small African kingdom of Swaziland when the food supply dried up. There were too many elephants, endangered rhinos and other animals to feed, so the parks decided they needed to remove about half of their elephant herd. The Henry Doorly Zoo & Aquarium and zoos in Dallas and Wichita, Kansas, volunteered to take the elephants and stepped in to care for and feed the animals while they waited to travel to America. The zoos also promised to send $450,000 to the African parks to help care for their rhinos.

In March, the elephants were loaded into crates and onto a huge airplane. Veterinarians stayed with them for the entire 36-hour trip. First, five elephants were unloaded off the plane in Dallas, then six in Wichita. Finally, their last stop was at Omaha's Eppley Airfield. People lined the streets of Omaha's Old Market to welcome the elephants, who traveled in crates on a trailer down 10th and 13th Streets to the zoo.

Omaha's six elephants — five females and one male — stayed in their new home, the largest herd room in North America, for almost a month while doctors checked on them. More than 100 people lined up at the zoo to see the elephants when they were finally ready for their debut in their new building. Later, they went outside to play in the mud for the first time. Now, they have a yard for themselves, plus a huge space to share with zebras, impalas and guineafowl, complete with a pool, plenty of hay and a lot more. They're the zoo's first elephants since Shenga left for Cleveland in 2011.

The story behind LoLo's name

The zoo's littlest giraffe was the last one born in the old Giraffe Complex. The baby giraffe weighed 138 pounds and measured 6 feet tall when she was born November 4, 2014.

The zoo asked people to submit their own ideas for her name, and one stood out. Almost 700 people — more than one-fourth of the total entries — requested "LoLo." The inspiration was a then-12-year-old girl named Lauren "LoLo" Hacker, who at the time was fighting a rare form of cancer called acute myelocytic leukemia, subtype monoblastic. While she was in the hospital, her friends, family and classmates filled her room with stuffed animal giraffes — her favorite animal. She had so many — 56 — that the hospital staff called her room "the giraffe suite."

LoLo's friends and family asked people on Facebook and Instagram to submit the name "LoLo" for the naming contest. Zookeepers saw the list of names and chose LoLo, saying it fit the giraffe's personality.

The Henry Doorly Zoo & Aquarium's African Grasslands exhibit features 24 animal species:

LEOPARD TORTOISE
Scientific name: *Stigmochelys pardalis*
Conservation status: Least concern
Location: Rock Kopje
At the zoo: Since 2015

RETICULATED GIRAFFE
Scientific name: *Giraffa camelopardalis reticulata*
Conservation status: Least concern
Location: North mixed species habitat
At the zoo: Since 1975

KENYA CRESTED GUINEAFOWL
Scientific name: *Guttera pucherani*
Conservation status: Least concern
Location: Rock Kopje
At the zoo: Since 2014

WHITE RHINOCEROS
Scientific name: *Ceratotherium simum*
Conservation status: Near threatened
Location: North mixed species habitat
At the zoo: Since 1966

MEERKAT
Scientific name: *Suricata suricatta*
Conservation status: Least concern
Location: Rock Kopje
At the zoo: 1966-1967; since 2001

WHITE STORK
Scientific name: *Ciconia ciconia*
Conservation status: Least concern
Location: North mixed species habitat
At the zoo: Since 1983

ROCK HYRAX
Scientific name: *Procavia capensis*
Conservation status: Least concern
Location: Rock Kopje
At the zoo: Since 1999

SPUR-WINGED GOOSE
Scientific name: *Plectropterus gambensis*
Conservation status: Least concern
Location: North mixed species habitat
At the zoo: 1972-1974; since 1984

KLIPSPRINGER
Scientific name: *Oreotragus oreotragus*
Conservation status: Least concern
Location: Rock Kopje
At the zoo: Since 2001

OSTRICH
Scientific name: *Struthio camelus*
Conservation status: Least concern
Location: North mixed species habitat
At the zoo: Since 1972

WHITE-THROATED MONITOR LIZARD
Scientific name: *Varanus albigularis*
Conservation status: Least concern
Location: Rock Kopje
At the zoo: Since 2002

IMPALA
Scientific name: *Aepyceros melampus*
Conservation status: Least concern
Location: North and south mixed species habitat
At the zoo: Since 2015

AFRICAN ELEPHANT
Scientific name: *Loxodonta africana*
Conservation status: Vulnerable
Location: South mixed species habitat
At the zoo: 1966-2011; since 2016

PINK-BACKED PELICAN
Scientific name: *Pelecanus rufescens*
Conservation status: Least concern
Location: Lagoon
At the zoo: Since 2015

PLAINS ZEBRA
Scientific name: *Equus quagga*
Conservation status: Least concern
Location: South mixed species habitat
At the zoo: 1973-1986; since 2015

AFRICAN LION
Scientific name: *Panthera leo*
Conservation status: Vulnerable
Location: East of the lagoon
At the zoo: Since 1965

HELMETED GUINEAFOWL
Scientific name: *Numida meleagris*
Conservation status: Least concern
Location: South mixed species habitat
At the zoo: Since 2015

CHEETAH
Scientific name: *Acinonyx jubatus*
Conservation status: Vulnerable
Location: East of the lagoon
At the zoo: 1965-1991; since 2001

EGYPTIAN GOOSE
Scientific name: *Alopochen aegyptiaca*
Conservation status: Least concern
Location: South mixed species habitat
At the zoo: Since 1974

BONGO
Scientific name: *Tragelaphus eurycerus*
Conservation status: Near threatened
Location: East of the lagoon
At the zoo: Since 2001

AFRICAN PYGMY GOAT
Scientific name: *Capra hircus*
Conservation status: Not listed (stable)
Location: Pygmy goat kraal
At the zoo: Since the 1960s

AFRICAN SPURRED TORTOISE
Scientific name: *Centrochelys sulcata*
Conservation status: Vulnerable
Location: East of the lagoon
At the zoo: 1999-2013; since 2015

WHITE-FACED WHISTLING DUCK
Scientific name: *Dendrocygna viduata*
Conservation status: Least concern
Location: Lagoon
At the zoo: 1992-2007; since 2014

SABLE ANTELOPE
Scientific name: *Hippotragus niger*
Conservation status: Least concern
Location: East of the lagoon
At the zoo: Since 1965

BY CHRIS PETERS OF THE OMAHA WORLD-HERALD
WITH PHOTOS BY MEGAN FARMER, BRENDAN SULLIVAN AND KENT SIEVERS

Editor: Dan Sullivan   **Designer:** Christine Zueck-Watkins   **Photo Imaging:** Jolene McHugh

Contributing Editors: Sara Ziegler, Pam Thomas, Kathy Sullivan

Print & Production Coordinators: Pat "Murphy" Benoit, Bryan Kroenke

Intellectual Property Manager: Michelle Gullett   **Director of Marketing:** Rich Warren

Executive Editor: Mike Reilly   **President and Publisher:** Terry Kroeger

SPECIAL THANKS:

Dennis Pate: zoo director and CEO

Dawn Ream: communications & marketing director

Andrea Hennings: community engagement manager

Dan Cassidy: general curator

The entire hoofstock staff at the Henry Doorly Zoo & Aquarium, including keepers **Cole Mapes, Kelly Goodyear,**
Emmy Fortina-Neuman, Josh Shandera, Jami Guernsey, Larry Nuzum Jr. and **Mike Benner;**
lead hoofstock keepers **Arden Brewer** and **Eric Johnson;** and hoofstock supervisor **Jack Hetherington**

Desert Dome staffers **Kristi McGrath,** senior keeper, and **Lindsay Sears,** supervisor

Andy Reeves, senior keeper of reptiles and amphibians

Cats and bears staff **Jenna Kocourek,** senior keeper, and **Mike "Rocky" Verbrigghe,** lead keeper

Jordan Anderson, interactive animal programs keeper

Birds staff **Bob Lastovica,** supervisor; **Tim Shaw,** lead keeper; and **Jess Conroy,** senior keeper

Lee G. Simmons Conservation Park and Wildlife Safari staff **Joe Shepard,**
assistant superintendent, and **Tony Gates,** senior keeper

Omaha World-Herald • 1314 Douglas St. Omaha, NE 68102-1811

First Edition ISBN: 978-0-692-74658-5 • Printed by Walsworth Publishing Co. • Marceline, MO